PRINCEWILL LAGANG

21st Century Entrepreneurial Trends and Predictions

First published by PRINCEWILL LAGANG 2023

Copyright © 2023 by Princewill Lagang

All rights reserved. No part of this publication may be reproduced, stored or transmitted in any form or by any means, electronic, mechanical, photocopying, recording, scanning, or otherwise without written permission from the publisher. It is illegal to copy this book, post it to a website, or distribute it by any other means without permission.

Princewill Lagang asserts the moral right to be identified as the author of this work.

First edition

This book was professionally typeset on Reedsy.
Find out more at reedsy.com

Contents

1. 21st Century Entrepreneurial Trends and Predictions — 1
2. Navigating the Digital Frontier — 6
3. The Rise of Social Entrepreneurship — 9
4. Thriving in the Gig Economy — 12
5. Sustainability and Green Entrepreneurship — 15
6. Embracing Artificial Intelligence and Automation — 18
7. Navigating the Global Business Landscape — 21
8. The Art of Leadership in Entrepreneurship — 24
9. Funding and Financing Your Entrepreneurial Venture — 27
10. Scaling and Sustaining Your Entrepreneurial Venture — 30
11. Crisis Management and Resilience in Entrepreneurship — 33
12. Entrepreneurship in a Changing World: Trends and Challenges — 36
13. Summary — 39

1

21st Century Entrepreneurial Trends and Predictions

In the ever-evolving landscape of business and commerce, the 21st century has brought forth a dynamic and transformative era for entrepreneurs. With the rapid advancement of technology, shifting societal values, and global challenges, entrepreneurship has become a key driver of innovation, economic growth, and social change. This chapter delves into the entrepreneurial trends and predictions that have defined the 21st century, shedding light on the exciting opportunities and challenges awaiting those with the vision and determination to shape the future.

1.1 The Digital Revolution:

At the heart of the 21st-century entrepreneurial landscape is the digital revolution. The advent of the internet and its subsequent evolution has revolutionized the way business is conducted, paving the way for new avenues of entrepreneurship. Today, entrepreneurs no longer need a physical storefront to reach their customers. E-commerce platforms, mobile apps, and online marketplaces have become the new shopfronts. This shift has given rise to a generation of digital natives who leverage technology to create, market, and distribute products and services in ways that were unimaginable just a few decades ago.

The proliferation of e-commerce platforms like Amazon, the rise of tech startups like Uber and Airbnb, and the growth of social media giants like Facebook have reshaped entire industries. With the Internet of Things (IoT), blockchain, and artificial intelligence (AI) technologies continually advancing, the digital revolution shows no signs of slowing down. In the 21st century, entrepreneurs must not only be tech-savvy but also prepared to adapt and innovate in an environment that is constantly evolving.

1.2 The Rise of Social Entrepreneurship:

The 21st century has witnessed a significant shift in societal values, with a growing emphasis on sustainability, social responsibility, and ethical business practices. This shift has given rise to the phenomenon of social entrepreneurship, where individuals and organizations aim to address pressing global issues while also turning a profit. It's no longer enough for businesses to focus solely on profit; consumers increasingly demand that companies take an active role in addressing social and environmental challenges.

Enterprises like Patagonia, TOMS, and Warby Parker have successfully integrated social and environmental responsibility into their business models. They demonstrate that a commitment to social and environmental causes can not only be profitable but also a powerful marketing tool. In the 21st century, entrepreneurs who embrace the principles of social entrepreneurship have a unique opportunity to make a positive impact on the world while building a sustainable business.

1.3 The Gig Economy and Freelancing:

The 21st century has seen a dramatic shift in the nature of work, with the rise of the gig economy and freelancing. Traditional employment models are being challenged by a growing desire for flexibility and independence. Entrepreneurial-minded individuals are seizing the opportunity to work on their terms, providing a wide range of services from graphic design to consulting to ride-sharing.

Digital platforms like Upwork, Fiverr, and Uber have democratized access to work, enabling anyone with a skill to market themselves and find clients worldwide. While the gig economy offers newfound flexibility, it also presents challenges such as job security and access to benefits. Entrepreneurs who navigate this shifting landscape will play a vital role in shaping the future of work.

1.4 Sustainability and Green Entrepreneurship:

As environmental concerns take center stage, sustainable and green entrepreneurship is on the rise. Climate change, resource scarcity, and pollution have created a sense of urgency to develop eco-friendly solutions. Entrepreneurs are stepping up to create innovative products and services that minimize environmental impact. From renewable energy startups to companies focusing on reducing waste and recycling, the green economy is growing rapidly.

Investors and consumers alike are increasingly supporting businesses that prioritize sustainability. Entrepreneurs who lead the charge in this arena are not only contributing to a healthier planet but also tapping into a market with significant growth potential.

1.5 Artificial Intelligence and Automation:

The integration of artificial intelligence and automation is a trend that has the potential to revolutionize various industries. While these technologies offer immense possibilities for improving efficiency and reducing costs, they also bring concerns about job displacement. Entrepreneurs in the 21st century must harness the power of AI and automation to gain a competitive edge while being mindful of the broader societal implications.

Predictive analytics, robotics, and machine learning are just a few of the areas where entrepreneurs are making waves. Those who navigate the ethical and societal dimensions of AI and automation will be well-positioned for success in this brave new world.

1.6 Globalization and Cross-Border Entrepreneurship:

In the 21st century, the world has become a global marketplace. E-commerce, improved transportation, and digital communication have made it easier than ever to do business across borders. Entrepreneurs who understand the intricacies of international markets and adapt to the demands of a global customer base have the potential to tap into new revenue streams and reach a broader audience.

As international trade barriers evolve, entrepreneurs must also navigate shifting geopolitical landscapes and changing regulations. However, those who successfully bridge cultures and expand their businesses globally can experience unparalleled growth and success.

1.7 Conclusion:

The 21st century presents entrepreneurs with a unique set of challenges and opportunities. From the digital revolution to the rise of social entrepreneurship, from the gig economy to the imperative of sustainability, and from the integration of AI and automation to the possibilities of global expansion, the entrepreneurial landscape is continually evolving. Those who stay informed, adapt, and embrace these trends will be well-prepared to thrive in this exciting and dynamic century of entrepreneurship. The chapters that follow will delve deeper into each of these trends, providing insights, case studies, and actionable strategies for aspiring and established entrepreneurs alike.

2

Navigating the Digital Frontier

2.1 Introduction: The Digital Revolution's Impact on Entrepreneurship

The digital revolution has been a game-changer for entrepreneurs in the 21st century. In this chapter, we will explore how technology has transformed the entrepreneurial landscape, offering new opportunities and challenges. From e-commerce to digital marketing, from data analytics to remote work, we will delve into the ways in which technology has reshaped the entrepreneurial journey.

2.2 E-Commerce and Online Marketplaces

One of the most profound changes in entrepreneurship has been the explosive growth of e-commerce. Traditional brick-and-mortar stores now share the retail landscape with online marketplaces like Amazon and platforms like Shopify. This section will explore the rise of e-commerce, its impact on consumer behavior, and the keys to success in the online marketplace.

2.3 Digital Marketing and Social Media

In the age of digital entrepreneurship, marketing has shifted from traditional methods to the digital realm. Entrepreneurs must understand the power of social media, content marketing, SEO, and pay-per-click advertising. We will delve into the strategies and tactics that can help entrepreneurs effectively navigate the digital marketing landscape.

2.4 Data Analytics and Business Intelligence

Data is the new gold in the digital age, and entrepreneurs who harness its power gain a significant advantage. We will explore the role of data analytics, big data, and business intelligence in decision-making, customer insights, and improving operational efficiency.

2.5 Remote Work and Virtual Teams

The 21st century has witnessed a significant shift towards remote work and virtual teams. The COVID-19 pandemic accelerated this trend, but it was already well underway. Entrepreneurs must now adapt to leading and managing teams in a digital environment. This section will provide insights into the challenges and opportunities of remote work and best practices for virtual team collaboration.

2.6 Cybersecurity and Digital Risks

With the increasing reliance on digital technologies, entrepreneurs face new risks, especially in terms of cybersecurity. Protecting sensitive data and maintaining the trust of customers is paramount. This section will explore the threats and best practices for safeguarding digital assets.

2.7 Innovation and Technology Adoption

Embracing innovation is critical in the digital age. Entrepreneurs need to stay updated with the latest technological advancements and adapt their business models accordingly. We'll discuss the innovation mindset, technology adoption, and how to stay at the forefront of your industry.

2.8 The Future of Digital Entrepreneurship

As we conclude this chapter, we'll take a glimpse into the future of digital entrepreneurship. The trends, technologies, and strategies that will shape the entrepreneurial landscape in the coming years, and how entrepreneurs can prepare for what lies ahead.

This chapter aims to provide a comprehensive understanding of how the digital revolution has influenced entrepreneurship in the 21st century. From e-commerce to digital marketing, remote work to cybersecurity, it explores the opportunities and challenges presented by the digital frontier, and offers insights and strategies for success in this ever-evolving digital landscape.

3

The Rise of Social Entrepreneurship

3.1 Introduction: Redefining Success in the 21st Century

Social entrepreneurship is a powerful movement that has gained momentum in the 21st century. In this chapter, we will explore the intersection of business and social impact, as entrepreneurs increasingly seek to make a positive difference while pursuing profit. We'll examine the principles of social entrepreneurship, the motivations driving this movement, and the impact it has on both society and business.

3.2 Defining Social Entrepreneurship

This section will define social entrepreneurship and distinguish it from traditional entrepreneurship. We'll explore the fundamental concepts, such as the "double bottom line" and the "triple bottom line," which emphasize not only financial returns but also social and environmental outcomes.

3.3 The Motivation Behind Social Entrepreneurship

What drives individuals to become social entrepreneurs? This part of the chapter will delve into the motivations, values, and personal stories of social entrepreneurs. We'll explore the desire to address societal challenges, make a difference, and create sustainable solutions.

3.4 Successful Social Entrepreneurship Ventures

This section will showcase real-world examples of successful social entrepreneurship ventures. Case studies from organizations like Grameen Bank, The Bill and Melinda Gates Foundation, and BRAC will highlight innovative approaches to addressing poverty, healthcare, education, and other pressing global issues.

3.5 Measuring Impact: Metrics and Evaluation

Social entrepreneurship is all about creating positive change. In this part, we'll discuss the challenges and methods of measuring the social impact of these ventures. Key performance indicators (KPIs), impact assessment tools, and best practices for evaluating social outcomes will be explored.

3.6 The Challenges and Criticisms of Social Entrepreneurship

While social entrepreneurship is gaining traction, it is not without its challenges and critics. We will examine issues like financial sustainability, impact measurement, and concerns about mission drift. Addressing these challenges is vital for the long-term success of social entrepreneurship.

3.7 Funding and Investment in Social Entrepreneurship

Access to capital is a critical factor for any entrepreneurial venture, and social entrepreneurship is no exception. We will explore the funding landscape for social enterprises, including impact investing, grants, and crowdfunding. Additionally, we'll discuss how to attract and retain investors who share the vision of creating a better world.

3.8 The Future of Social Entrepreneurship

In the final section of this chapter, we will explore the future of social entrepreneurship. What trends are emerging, and how will they shape the movement in the coming years? How can social entrepreneurs continue to drive positive change and inspire the business world to adopt more socially responsible practices?

This chapter aims to provide a comprehensive understanding of social entrepreneurship, its principles, motivations, challenges, and impact. By examining successful cases, exploring impact measurement, and addressing the criticisms and funding landscape, it offers insights into how entrepreneurs can create businesses that drive positive social change in the 21st century.

4

Thriving in the Gig Economy

4.1 Introduction: The Gig Economy's Impact on Work and Entrepreneurship

The gig economy has disrupted traditional employment structures, offering individuals and entrepreneurs new avenues to work and generate income. In this chapter, we will explore the gig economy, what it means for workers and entrepreneurs, and how to succeed in this dynamic and flexible work landscape.

4.2 Defining the Gig Economy

This section will define the gig economy, shedding light on its characteristics, including short-term contracts, freelance work, and the use of digital platforms to connect workers with gigs. We will also discuss the various terms used to describe this phenomenon, such as the "on-demand economy" and "freelance economy."

4.3 The Rise of Freelancing and Independent Work

Freelancing is a fundamental aspect of the gig economy. This part of the chapter will delve into the reasons behind the rise of freelancing, examining the benefits and challenges it offers to both individuals and businesses.

4.4 Opportunities for Entrepreneurs in the Gig Economy

Entrepreneurs are not limited to traditional business structures. The gig economy offers ample opportunities for entrepreneurial-minded individuals to build businesses around the provision of goods and services in a gig-style format. We will explore various entrepreneurial paths in this section.

4.5 Challenges of the Gig Economy

While the gig economy provides flexibility, it also presents challenges, including income instability, limited access to benefits, and the absence of job security. We will delve into these challenges and provide strategies to address them.

4.6 Digital Platforms and Gig Work

The gig economy heavily relies on digital platforms and apps to connect workers with job opportunities. This section will discuss the role of platforms like Uber, Upwork, and TaskRabbit in facilitating gig work and how entrepreneurs can leverage such platforms to create new ventures.

4.7 Navigating the Legal Landscape

Gig work often blurs the lines between traditional employment and independent contracting, leading to legal and regulatory complexities. We will examine the legal considerations that entrepreneurs and gig workers should be aware of and provide guidance on compliance and risk management.

4.8 Building a Personal Brand and Reputation

In the gig economy, personal branding and reputation are essential. Entrepreneurs and gig workers alike can succeed by cultivating a strong online presence, garnering positive reviews, and establishing themselves as trustworthy and skilled professionals.

4.9 The Future of Work and Entrepreneurship in the Gig Economy

As we conclude this chapter, we will explore the future of work and entrepreneurship in the gig economy. What trends are emerging, and how will they shape the gig landscape in the coming years? How can individuals and entrepreneurs adapt and thrive in this evolving work environment?

This chapter aims to provide a comprehensive understanding of the gig economy, its impact on work and entrepreneurship, the opportunities it offers, and the challenges it presents. By exploring the legal landscape, personal branding, and the future of work, it offers insights and strategies for individuals and entrepreneurs seeking to succeed in the gig economy of the 21st century.

5

Sustainability and Green Entrepreneurship

5.1 Introduction: The Imperative of Sustainable Entrepreneurship

The 21st century has brought environmental concerns to the forefront, demanding a transformation in the way we do business. This chapter delves into sustainability and green entrepreneurship, exploring how entrepreneurs can address pressing environmental challenges while building profitable and responsible businesses.

5.2 Defining Green Entrepreneurship

We begin by defining green entrepreneurship and explaining its significance in the modern world. Green entrepreneurs prioritize environmental sustainability and social responsibility, aiming to reduce negative environmental impacts while creating economic value.

5.3 The Business Case for Sustainability

Sustainability is not just about saving the planet; it's also a sound business strategy. In this section, we will explore the compelling business case for sustainability, including cost savings, market opportunities, and risk mitigation.

5.4 Sustainable Innovation and Green Technologies

Green entrepreneurs are at the forefront of sustainable innovation, developing technologies and solutions that minimize environmental harm. We will delve into green technologies, renewable energy, and sustainable product design as essential elements of green entrepreneurship.

5.5 Circular Economy and Waste Reduction

The circular economy model, which focuses on reducing waste and reusing resources, is a key component of green entrepreneurship. We will discuss how entrepreneurs can implement circular economy principles to minimize waste and create sustainable business practices.

5.6 Impact Investing and Green Financing

Access to capital is crucial for green entrepreneurs. This section explores the world of impact investing, green financing, and grants, providing insights into how green entrepreneurs can secure funding for their environmentally responsible ventures.

5.7 Sustainability Reporting and Transparency

Transparency is a cornerstone of green entrepreneurship. Entrepreneurs must communicate their sustainability efforts to gain the trust of customers and investors. We will discuss sustainability reporting, certifications, and transparency best practices.

5.8 Navigating Regulatory and Compliance Challenges

Green entrepreneurs often face a complex web of regulations and compliance requirements. We will explore the legal considerations, environmental standards, and certifications that entrepreneurs must navigate to ensure they meet sustainability goals.

5.9 The Future of Green Entrepreneurship

As we conclude this chapter, we will take a look at the future of green entrepreneurship. What trends are emerging, and how will they shape the green business landscape in the coming years? How can green entrepreneurs continue to drive positive environmental change and inspire the broader business community to adopt more sustainable practices?

This chapter aims to provide a comprehensive understanding of sustainability and green entrepreneurship, its significance, the business case for it, innovative solutions, and the challenges faced. By exploring the circular economy, impact investing, and the future of green entrepreneurship, it offers insights and strategies for entrepreneurs seeking to build environmentally responsible businesses in the 21st century.

6

Embracing Artificial Intelligence and Automation

6.1 Introduction: The AI and Automation Revolution

The integration of artificial intelligence (AI) and automation is reshaping industries and entrepreneurial opportunities. In this chapter, we explore how AI and automation are transforming businesses, driving innovation, and creating new challenges and possibilities for entrepreneurs.

6.2 Understanding Artificial Intelligence and Automation

We begin by defining artificial intelligence and automation, explaining their fundamental concepts, and distinguishing between different forms of AI, such as machine learning and deep learning.

6.3 The Impact of AI and Automation on Entrepreneurship

The rise of AI and automation offers entrepreneurs the potential to streamline operations, enhance customer experiences, and create innovative products and services. We explore how these technologies are influencing various industries and discuss the advantages they bring to entrepreneurial endeavors.

6.4 AI-Driven Decision Making and Predictive Analytics

Entrepreneurs can harness AI to make data-driven decisions and leverage predictive analytics to anticipate market trends and customer behaviors. This section explores the power of AI in decision-making and how predictive analytics can provide a competitive edge.

6.5 Robotics and Automation in Manufacturing and Services

AI-driven robotics and automation are revolutionizing manufacturing and service industries. Entrepreneurs are adopting these technologies to increase efficiency and reduce costs. We delve into examples, benefits, and challenges in implementing robotics and automation.

6.6 Ethical and Societal Considerations

The adoption of AI and automation comes with ethical and societal implications, including job displacement and bias in algorithms. We discuss the importance of addressing these concerns and adopting responsible AI practices in entrepreneurial ventures.

6.7 Human-AI Collaboration

Entrepreneurs are increasingly exploring ways to collaborate with AI, combining human creativity and problem-solving with AI's computational power. We examine how this synergy can drive innovation and competitive advantage.

6.8 Entrepreneurial Opportunities in AI and Automation

Entrepreneurial opportunities abound in AI and automation, from developing AI-driven products and services to creating AI-powered startups. We provide insights into how entrepreneurs can identify and seize opportunities in this field.

6.9 Preparing for the AI-Driven Future

As we conclude this chapter, we explore how entrepreneurs can prepare for the AI-driven future. What skills and knowledge are essential, and how can entrepreneurs stay ahead in a rapidly evolving technological landscape?

This chapter aims to provide a comprehensive understanding of the impact of artificial intelligence and automation on entrepreneurship. By exploring the potential applications, ethical considerations, and entrepreneurial opportunities, it offers insights and strategies for entrepreneurs looking to leverage AI and automation in their ventures in the 21st century.

7

Navigating the Global Business Landscape

7.1 Introduction: The Globalization of Entrepreneurship

In the 21st century, entrepreneurship is no longer confined by borders. This chapter explores the opportunities and challenges of doing business on a global scale. We'll examine the impact of globalization, the potential benefits of expanding internationally, and the strategies entrepreneurs can use to navigate the global business landscape.

7.2 Understanding Globalization

We begin by defining globalization and exploring its various facets, including the flow of goods, services, information, and capital across borders. Understanding the interconnected nature of today's global economy is essential for entrepreneurs venturing into the international arena.

7.3 The Advantages of Going Global

Global expansion offers numerous advantages for entrepreneurs, including access to larger markets, diversification of risks, and opportunities for growth.

This section delves into the benefits and potential rewards of taking a business global.

7.4 Navigating Cultural Differences

Entrepreneurs engaging in international business must be sensitive to cultural nuances and differences. This part of the chapter will discuss how to navigate cultural diversity and adapt business strategies to meet the expectations of diverse customer bases and workforces.

7.5 Legal and Regulatory Challenges

Expanding into international markets comes with legal and regulatory complexities. We'll explore the challenges entrepreneurs may face, including compliance with foreign laws, intellectual property protection, and trade restrictions.

7.6 Market Entry Strategies

Entrepreneurs have various strategies at their disposal when entering global markets, such as exporting, franchising, joint ventures, and mergers and acquisitions. We'll discuss the pros and cons of each strategy and provide guidance on selecting the most appropriate approach.

7.7 Currency and Financial Considerations

Fluctuations in currency exchange rates can have a significant impact on global business operations. This section will delve into currency risk management, international financial planning, and the importance of managing currency exposure.

7.8 Global Marketing and Branding

Marketing on a global scale requires a nuanced approach. We'll explore global marketing strategies, the adaptation of branding and messaging, and the use of digital tools to reach international audiences effectively.

7.9 The Future of Global Entrepreneurship

In the final part of this chapter, we'll discuss the future of global entrepreneurship. What trends are emerging, and how will they shape the global business landscape in the coming years? How can entrepreneurs prepare for the challenges and opportunities that lie ahead in an increasingly interconnected world?

This chapter aims to provide a comprehensive understanding of global entrepreneurship, its advantages, cultural challenges, legal complexities, market entry strategies, and financial considerations. By exploring global marketing, currency management, and the future of global entrepreneurship, it offers insights and strategies for entrepreneurs seeking to thrive in the global business landscape of the 21st century.

8

The Art of Leadership in Entrepreneurship

8.1 Introduction: The Role of Leadership in Entrepreneurship

Effective leadership is the cornerstone of entrepreneurial success. In this chapter, we explore the essential role of leadership in guiding ventures to success, fostering innovation, and navigating the challenges of entrepreneurship in the 21st century.

8.2 Defining Entrepreneurial Leadership

We begin by defining entrepreneurial leadership, highlighting the unique qualities and skills that distinguish it from other forms of leadership. Entrepreneurial leaders are visionaries, risk-takers, and agents of change.

8.3 Leadership Styles and Approaches

Entrepreneurial leaders may adopt various leadership styles, from transformational to servant leadership. We delve into the strengths and weaknesses of different approaches and discuss when and how to apply them in the entrepreneurial context.

8.4 Vision and Strategy

An entrepreneurial leader must articulate a clear vision and develop a strategic plan to achieve it. This section explores the importance of vision, mission statements, and strategic planning in guiding the business forward.

8.5 Team Building and Talent Management

Building and managing a talented and motivated team is crucial for entrepreneurial success. We discuss strategies for recruiting, retaining, and developing top talent, as well as fostering a positive organizational culture.

8.6 Adaptability and Resilience

Entrepreneurial journeys are often fraught with uncertainty and adversity. We examine the importance of adaptability and resilience in the face of challenges and setbacks, and how leaders can cultivate these traits.

8.7 Decision-Making and Risk Management

Entrepreneurial leaders must make critical decisions and manage risks. We explore decision-making models, risk assessment, and strategies for mitigating potential challenges and uncertainties.

8.8 Communication and Conflict Resolution

Effective communication is a cornerstone of leadership. We discuss communication strategies, including active listening and conflict resolution, to foster positive relationships and resolve disputes within the organization.

8.9 Ethical Leadership and Social Responsibility

In the modern world, ethical leadership and social responsibility are paramount. We delve into the ethical considerations of leadership, including corporate social responsibility, and the impact of ethical leadership on organizational success and reputation.

8.10 The Future of Entrepreneurial Leadership

In the concluding part of this chapter, we consider the future of entrepreneurial leadership. What trends are emerging, and how will they shape leadership in entrepreneurship in the coming years? How can entrepreneurial leaders prepare for the challenges and opportunities on the horizon in the 21st century?

This chapter aims to provide a comprehensive understanding of the art of leadership in entrepreneurship. By exploring leadership styles, vision and strategy, team building, adaptability, ethical leadership, and the future of entrepreneurial leadership, it offers insights and strategies for aspiring and established entrepreneurial leaders to thrive in the dynamic landscape of the 21st century.

9

Funding and Financing Your Entrepreneurial Venture

9.1 Introduction: The Financial Landscape of Entrepreneurship

Financing is the lifeblood of entrepreneurial ventures. In this chapter, we will explore the various funding options and strategies available to entrepreneurs in the 21st century, guiding you through the process of securing the financial resources necessary for your business.

9.2 Bootstrapping and Self-Funding

Many entrepreneurs start their journeys by self-funding their ventures, a practice known as bootstrapping. We'll discuss the advantages and limitations of this approach, as well as the strategies for making the most of your own resources.

9.3 Personal Savings and Family & Friends

Personal savings and contributions from family and friends are common sources of initial capital for entrepreneurs. This section will provide guidance on navigating these relationships and managing financial expectations.

9.4 Angel Investors and Seed Funding

Angel investors and seed funding provide early-stage financing for startups. We'll explore how to attract angel investors, what they look for in investment opportunities, and the terms and conditions typically associated with seed funding.

9.5 Venture Capital and Equity Financing

Venture capital is a prominent source of financing for high-growth startups. We'll discuss the venture capital landscape, the process of securing venture capital, and the implications of equity financing on ownership and control.

9.6 Crowdfunding and Alternative Financing

The rise of crowdfunding platforms has opened new doors for entrepreneurs to raise capital from a diverse pool of backers. We'll explore the crowdfunding model and other alternative financing options, such as peer-to-peer lending and revenue-based financing.

9.7 Small Business Loans and Grants

Small business loans and grants offered by government agencies and private organizations provide accessible funding options for entrepreneurs. This section will delve into the types of loans and grants available, the application process, and how to improve your chances of securing them.

9.8 Corporate Partnerships and Strategic Alliances

Entrepreneurs can forge strategic partnerships and alliances with corporations to access resources and capital. We'll discuss the advantages and challenges of these arrangements and provide insights into building mutually beneficial relationships.

9.9 Pitching and Presenting Your Business

Securing funding often hinges on an entrepreneur's ability to pitch their business idea effectively. We'll explore the art of pitching, including crafting a compelling business plan, perfecting your elevator pitch, and delivering a persuasive presentation to potential investors.

9.10 Managing and Allocating Funds

Once funding is secured, efficient financial management is essential. We'll discuss strategies for budgeting, allocating funds, tracking expenses, and maintaining financial transparency.

9.11 The Future of Entrepreneurial Financing

In the final part of this chapter, we'll consider the future of entrepreneurial financing. What trends are emerging, and how will they shape the financing landscape for entrepreneurs in the coming years? How can entrepreneurs stay ahead in an ever-evolving world of financing options?

This chapter aims to provide a comprehensive understanding of financing options and strategies for entrepreneurial ventures. By exploring bootstrapping, angel investment, venture capital, crowdfunding, and the future of entrepreneurial financing, it offers insights and strategies for entrepreneurs seeking to secure the financial resources needed for success in the 21st century.

10

Scaling and Sustaining Your Entrepreneurial Venture

10.1 Introduction: The Journey of Scaling and Sustaining

Scaling a business while maintaining sustainability is a crucial phase in an entrepreneurial venture's evolution. In this chapter, we explore the strategies, challenges, and critical considerations for entrepreneurs looking to expand their businesses and ensure long-term viability.

10.2 The Importance of Scalability

We begin by emphasizing the significance of scalability in entrepreneurship. Understanding what scalability means, why it matters, and when to consider scaling are pivotal steps in this journey.

10.3 Strategies for Growth and Expansion

Entrepreneurs must identify effective strategies for growth and expansion. We delve into organic growth, strategic partnerships, mergers and acquisitions, franchising, and other avenues to scale a business successfully.

10.4 Building and Managing Teams

Scaling a business often requires building and managing larger teams. We discuss the intricacies of recruiting, onboarding, and leading teams as the business grows.

10.5 Marketing and Branding for Expansion

Marketing plays a pivotal role in scaling a business. We explore the strategies, tactics, and branding considerations that entrepreneurs need to address when expanding their reach to new markets and audiences.

10.6 Operational Efficiency and Technology Integration

As businesses scale, operational efficiency becomes a key concern. We'll discuss the role of technology in improving operational processes, reducing costs, and increasing productivity.

10.7 Financial Management and Access to Capital

Securing the necessary financial resources is essential for scaling. We explore options for accessing capital, managing financial resources, and building relationships with investors and lenders.

10.8 Overcoming Growth Challenges

Scaling is not without its challenges. We'll discuss the common hurdles entrepreneurs face during the growth phase and provide strategies for overcoming them.

10.9 Maintaining Sustainability and Long-Term Viability

While growth is essential, sustainability is equally critical. We'll explore how to ensure the long-term viability of a business by implementing sustainability practices and responsible management.

10.10 Exit Strategies and Future Directions

At some point, entrepreneurs may consider exit strategies, such as selling the business or transitioning to new ventures. We'll discuss exit planning and how to make strategic decisions about the future direction of your entrepreneurial journey.

10.11 The Future of Scaling and Sustaining

In the concluding part of this chapter, we'll consider the future of scaling and sustaining entrepreneurial ventures. What trends are emerging, and how will they shape the scaling and sustainability landscape for entrepreneurs in the coming years? How can entrepreneurs prepare for the challenges and opportunities on the horizon in the 21st century?

This chapter aims to provide a comprehensive understanding of scaling and sustaining entrepreneurial ventures. By exploring strategies for growth, team management, financial considerations, and the future of scaling and sustaining, it offers insights and strategies for entrepreneurs seeking to expand their businesses while maintaining long-term success.

11

Crisis Management and Resilience in Entrepreneurship

11.1 Introduction: Navigating the Storms of Entrepreneurship

Crisis is an inherent part of entrepreneurship. In this chapter, we explore the strategies, skills, and mindset needed to manage and navigate through crises, whether they be financial downturns, market shifts, or unforeseen disruptions. Resilience and crisis management are essential for the longevity of entrepreneurial ventures.

11.2 Understanding Entrepreneurial Resilience

We begin by defining entrepreneurial resilience and its importance. Resilience involves the ability to adapt, recover, and thrive in the face of adversity. Entrepreneurs must develop this skill to weather challenges successfully.

11.3 Identifying and Preparing for Potential Crises

Proactive crisis management begins with identifying potential crises. We'll discuss how to anticipate and prepare for crises, creating contingency plans and ensuring business continuity.

11.4 Crisis Communication and Stakeholder Management

Effective crisis communication is crucial. We explore the importance of transparency, timely communication, and stakeholder management in maintaining trust and reputation during challenging times.

11.5 Financial Resilience and Risk Mitigation

Financial resilience involves managing risks and securing the financial stability of the business. We discuss strategies for financial planning, risk mitigation, and ensuring the business's sustainability during crises.

11.6 Adapting and Innovating in Times of Crisis

Crisis often demands adaptability and innovation. Entrepreneurs must be ready to pivot and find new opportunities amidst adversity. We delve into strategies for adapting to changing circumstances and fostering innovation during crises.

11.7 Emotional and Mental Resilience

Crisis management also requires emotional and mental resilience. We'll discuss strategies for maintaining a positive mindset, managing stress, and seeking support during challenging times.

11.8 Learning from Crisis: Post-Crisis Evaluation and Recovery

Once a crisis has passed, it's essential to evaluate what went wrong and what can be improved. We explore the post-crisis phase, discussing recovery strategies, and applying lessons learned to strengthen the business.

11.9 Building a Resilient Organizational Culture

A resilient organizational culture is essential for navigating crises. We discuss how to build a culture that values adaptability, transparency, and teamwork in the face of adversity.

11.10 Crisis Simulations and Preparedness

Preparedness is key to effective crisis management. We explore crisis simulations and drills that can help entrepreneurs and their teams respond more effectively when actual crises occur.

11.11 The Future of Crisis Management and Resilience

In the concluding part of this chapter, we'll consider the future of crisis management and resilience in entrepreneurship. What trends are emerging, and how will they shape the landscape for entrepreneurs in the coming years? How can entrepreneurs prepare for the unforeseen challenges and uncertainties of the 21st century?

This chapter aims to provide a comprehensive understanding of crisis management and resilience in entrepreneurship. By exploring proactive crisis preparation, emotional resilience, post-crisis recovery, and the future of crisis management, it offers insights and strategies for entrepreneurs seeking to navigate the storms of entrepreneurship and emerge stronger on the other side.

12

Entrepreneurship in a Changing World: Trends and Challenges

12.1 Introduction: The Ever-Evolving Entrepreneurial Landscape

The entrepreneurial landscape is constantly changing. In this final chapter, we examine the dynamic trends, emerging challenges, and shifting paradigms that entrepreneurs must navigate in a rapidly evolving world. Understanding these changes is crucial for success in the 21st century.

12.2 Technological Advancements and Innovation

Technological advancements continue to shape entrepreneurship. We explore the latest technological trends, such as AI, blockchain, and biotechnology, and their impact on business opportunities and innovation.

12.3 Market Dynamics and Consumer Behavior

Market dynamics and consumer behavior are continually evolving. We discuss changing consumer preferences, the rise of e-commerce, and how entrepreneurs can adapt to shifting market trends.

12.4 Environmental and Sustainability Concerns

The world is becoming increasingly conscious of environmental and sustainability issues. We explore the growing importance of sustainable practices and how entrepreneurs can integrate eco-friendly approaches into their businesses.

12.5 Globalization and Geopolitical Challenges

Globalization has opened doors to new opportunities but also introduced geopolitical challenges. We discuss trade tensions, regulatory complexities, and the implications for international business.

12.6 Diversity, Equity, and Inclusion

Diversity, equity, and inclusion have gained prominence in the entrepreneurial world. We explore the importance of creating inclusive workplaces and serving diverse customer bases.

12.7 Health and Well-being in the Post-Pandemic Era

The COVID-19 pandemic has left a lasting impact on health and well-being considerations. We discuss how entrepreneurs can adapt to health-conscious consumer behaviors and maintain business continuity.

12.8 Legal and Ethical Considerations

Legal and ethical considerations are paramount. We explore data privacy regulations, ethical practices, and how entrepreneurs can navigate complex legal landscapes.

12.9 The Gig Economy and Remote Work Trends

The gig economy and remote work are becoming more prevalent. We discuss the implications of these trends for businesses and the workforce, as well as how to adapt to the changing nature of work.

12.10 Entrepreneurial Education and Skill Development

The need for entrepreneurial education and skill development is growing. We explore the importance of ongoing learning and skill enhancement to stay competitive in the entrepreneurial world.

12.11 The Future of Entrepreneurship

In the final part of this chapter, we'll consider the future of entrepreneurship. What trends are emerging, and how will they shape the entrepreneurial landscape in the coming years? How can entrepreneurs prepare for the challenges and opportunities of an ever-changing world?

This chapter aims to provide a comprehensive understanding of the dynamic trends and challenges in entrepreneurship. By exploring technology, market dynamics, sustainability, diversity, and the future of entrepreneurship, it offers insights and strategies for entrepreneurs looking to thrive in a world of constant change and innovation.

13

Summary

In this comprehensive book on 21st-century entrepreneurship, we have explored a wide range of topics to help entrepreneurs thrive in a rapidly changing world. Here's a brief summary of each chapter:

Chapter 1: "21st Century Entrepreneurial Trends and Predictions"
   - Explores the shifting landscape of entrepreneurship in the digital age.
   - Highlights the importance of adaptability and innovation.
   - Discusses future trends and predictions for entrepreneurial success.

Chapter 2: "Navigating the Digital Frontier"
   - Examines how technology has transformed entrepreneurship.
   - Covers e-commerce, digital marketing, data analytics, remote work, and cybersecurity.
   - Provides insights into staying at the forefront of the digital landscape.

Chapter 3: "The Rise of Social Entrepreneurship"
   - Discusses the emergence of social entrepreneurship.
   - Explores motivations, definitions, and successful examples.
   - Highlights the impact of social entrepreneurship on society and business.

Chapter 4: "Thriving in the Gig Economy"

- Delves into the gig economy and its impact on work and entrepreneurship.
- Discusses freelancing, digital platforms, and the challenges and opportunities in gig work.
- Explores strategies for success in the gig economy.

Chapter 5: "Sustainability and Green Entrepreneurship"
- Focuses on green entrepreneurship and its role in addressing environmental challenges.
- Explores the business case for sustainability, green technologies, and circular economy.
- Discusses impact investing, sustainability reporting, and ethical considerations.

Chapter 6: "Embracing Artificial Intelligence and Automation"
- Explores the integration of AI and automation in entrepreneurship.
- Covers AI-driven decision-making, robotics, and ethical concerns.
- Provides insights into leveraging AI and automation for business success.

Chapter 7: "Navigating the Global Business Landscape"
- Examines opportunities and challenges of doing business on a global scale.
- Discusses market entry strategies, cultural considerations, and regulatory challenges.
- Explores the future of global entrepreneurship.

Chapter 8: "The Art of Leadership in Entrepreneurship"
- Highlights the importance of leadership in entrepreneurial success.
- Covers leadership styles, vision, strategy, team building, and ethical leadership.
- Discusses the future of entrepreneurial leadership.

Chapter 9: "Funding and Financing Your Entrepreneurial Venture"
- Explores various funding options, including bootstrapping, angel invest-

SUMMARY

ment, and crowdfunding.
- Discusses small business loans, grants, and alternative financing.
- Provides insights into financial management and the future of entrepreneurial financing.

Chapter 10: "Scaling and Sustaining Your Entrepreneurial Venture"
- Discusses strategies for scaling a business while maintaining sustainability.
- Covers team management, marketing for expansion, and operational efficiency.
- Explores the future of scaling and sustaining entrepreneurial ventures.

Chapter 11: "Crisis Management and Resilience in Entrepreneurship"
- Focuses on the importance of crisis management and resilience.
- Discusses crisis preparedness, communication, financial resilience, and emotional resilience.
- Explores crisis simulations and preparedness.

Chapter 12: "Entrepreneurship in a Changing World: Trends and Challenges"
- Examines the ever-evolving entrepreneurial landscape, including technological advancements, market dynamics, and sustainability.
- Discusses diversity, equity, and inclusion, health considerations, and legal and ethical aspects.
- Explores the future of entrepreneurship in a changing world.

This book provides a comprehensive guide for entrepreneurs seeking success in the 21st century, covering a wide range of topics and offering valuable insights and strategies to navigate the challenges and opportunities in the dynamic entrepreneurial landscape.

www.ingramcontent.com/pod-product-compliance
Lightning Source LLC
LaVergne TN
LVHW012131070526
838202LV00056B/5954